A
GIFT BOOK
Of
Teddy Bears

A GIFT *Of* BOOK

Teddy Bears

ILLUSTRATED BY *Rosalie Upton*

WELDON
PUBLISHING

Contents

These jolly little Teddy Bears,
Who always love to play,
When hugged by little boys and girls,
They'll scare all gloom away.

The
Teddy Bear
is Born

The wonder is that the
Teddy Bear should have arrived
so late, for to us the cuddly
creature seems timeless.
Yet, as will be revealed,
the Teddy is really a child of
the twentieth century...

The Bear from Mississippi

On 14 November 1902, President Theodore Roosevelt of the United States was in the middle of settling a boundary dispute in the South when he was taken on a hunting expedition. "Teddy" Roosevelt was a keen hunter, but the story goes that on this occasion the animal they tracked down was only a small, helpless cub. The president spied him, took aim with his rifle, but did not fire. The newspapers took up the tale, and America smiled over the incident and their president's soft heart.

Cartoonist Clifford K. Berryman of the *Washington Evening Star* had fun depicting Roosevelt "Drawing the Line in Mississippi", and his image of this first "Teddy" bear won over America. In the following months, Teddy Bears became the cutest, most cuddly, most wanted creatures in every home. The president, who admired bears both in the wild and on the toyshelf, had accidentally started a new craze.

Furry Friends

In the nineteenth century in Germany there lived a toymaker named Margarete Steiff. A childhood disease had left her crippled, but with her sister's help she sewed for a living. Her first success as a toymaker was with a felt elephant made into a pincushion, and by 1893 she was exhibiting a range of toy animals at the Leipzig Fair. Her nephew Richard first thought of the idea of a large bear with movable head and joints, made of mohair. Another nephew, Paul, tried to sell these bears, but it was not until the Leipzig Fair of 1903 that success really came for the Steiff factory. The first Steiff bear was known as "Friend Petz", but these popular furry toys began to be imported into the American market, and soon became known as Teddy Bears to suit the new craze. The Steiff bears always carried a nickel button in one ear, with the symbol of Margarete's original toy elephant.

These delightful Bears show the true Steiff characteristics,
and are drawn from furry originals.

The Ideal Toy

Morris Michtom laid claim to being the first significant manufacturer of Teddy Bears in the United States. A Russian immigrant, he and his wife ran a small candy store in Brooklyn, and decided to sell Teddies as well, made from brown plush material with movable limbs and button eyes.

Eventually the new furry bears were a familiar sight in toyshop windows, and the Michtoms went on to found the Ideal Toy Corporation, which is still a major manufacturer.

Children today can long for a Teddy as fervently as they did in the early years of the century. It is surprising how many adults also elect the Teddy as the ideal companion throughout their lives.

The Bear in Britain

While Teddies were becoming the darlings of American homes, it so happened that England's Prince of Wales, the future Edward VII, was just cuddly and rounded enough to put one in mind of a portly Teddy Bear. Indeed, on a visit to the London Zoo in 1880, he himself had been lost in admiration for a furry koala, which everyone in those days thought of as a bear. To this day, toy koalas in Australia are known as "Teddy".

It was A.A. Milne who, in the nicest possible way, pointed out that the stout tummy which most self-respecting Teddies possess was shared by England's affable monarch, and the picture of Edward Bear admiring himself in a mirror, and dreaming of royal feasts, pomp and circumstance, is familiar to most British readers.

There is always something regal about a Teddy Bear: no matter how we treat our toy, he has his own dignity, his own secret life.

The Bear in Mythology

In the old, old stories,
bears were as close to us as
our parents, brothers and sisters,
and even a lover
could mysteriously slip
into a bear skin when
the gods willed ...

The Mighty Yu

Mountains and rivers, the haunts of bears, are constant themes in Chinese legends and art. When the earth was young, so they say, there lived a wonderful character, Yu. At the time of the great flood he used magic soil to build up mountains in the four corners of the world, so that they towered above the waters and steadied the earth with their weight. Later he achieved many miracles, directing watercourses on their way to the sea.

During each colossal labour, Yu took the shape of a yellow bear. His greatest feat was to remove Mount Hua from the path of the Yellow River. Gathering his huge strength, Yu pushed with his four paws and split the high mountain in half: the marks of his claws can be seen in the rock to this day.

At thirty, Yu married a woman from T'u-shan in the south, but never let her see his magical shape. Each time he was ready for her to bring him food, he beat a small drum and became her husband again. One day at work he let one rock fall against another, and at this drumlike sound his wife appeared. Terrified of the giant bear, she ran screaming away. Just as Yu caught up with her, she turned into a rock.

Restored to his own form, Yu pleaded with her to reappear, but for nine months she refused, until the day when the rock opened and their son K'i emerged, destined to become King of Hsia after his father.

Atalanta and the Mother Bear

Greek legend tells of a baby girl named Atalanta, whose father was so angry at not having a son that he had her taken up Mount Parthenion in Arcadia, and left to the elements.

A mother bear took pity on the tiny child and reared her with her own cubs, and for many years Atalanta lived surrounded by playful companions, under the protection of her strong, fierce mother. Perhaps she fell in love for ever with the outdoors, or perhaps the rough ways of the bear cubs stayed with her — whatever the reason, although she was later brought up by humans, Atalanta refused both house and husband, and spent her days running wild, hunting with her bow and spear.

Many were the suitors for her hand, but Atalanta challenged each to a foot race, then felled him with her spear as he ran ... until the day when the beautiful youth Melanion tricked her by dropping golden apples in her path, then winning the race when she stooped to pick them up.

An oracle had foretold that Atalanta would be changed into an animal if ever she married, but the bold girl was in love with Melanion, and accepted him with joy. So blissful

were the lovers that one day they forgot themselves and gave way to their desire in a sacred temple. At this crime, the great god Zeus struck out in anger and turned the couple into lions. Thus Atalanta lived out her days as she had begun, with the woods for her home, and at night a bed of soft leaves and a roof of stars.

Snow White and Rose Red

Two sisters once lived in a cottage in a wood, where their mother grew two rose bushes, a white one for beautiful Snow White and a crimson one for lovely Rose Red. One midwinter they took pity on a bear that begged for shelter, and every night it slept by their fire. In spring when their gentle friend departed, it tore its coat on the door, and the girls were puzzled to see gold shining beneath its fur.

Three times that summer Snow White and Rose Red came to the rescue of a greedy dwarf, who gave them nothing in return, though he had hordes of gold and jewels hidden in the forest. One day, just after they had saved the dwarf from a mighty eagle, the bear came upon the scene. The dwarf turned on the beast in fury, but with one cuff of its paw the bear silenced him for ever. Afraid, the girls turned away, but a sweet voice called them back: the rough bearskin had fallen to reveal a handsome prince, who had suffered all winter long under the dwarf's spell.

Snow White married the prince, Rose Red married his brother, and the rose bushes bloom still in the deep wood where first they met.

Jakob & Wilhelm Grimm

To Love a Teddy

*Who can explain the universal love
for the Teddy Bear?*

Arctophilia

An arctophile is someone who loves Teddies, especially one who collects them. Antique Teddies are bankable items, and very rare ones will fetch high prices at auction. There are people with rooms or houses full of them, who are still ready to pay thousands for yet another "treasure".

There is a great disparity between the fleeting pleasure these expensive Teddies give, and the world of joy that opens up when a child receives its first Teddy, one that may turn into a lifelong friend. A worn scrap of cloth with a button nose may figure more largely in a child's heart and imagination than all his or her other toys put together.

The Teddy Bear has its own value — and it has nothing to do with money.

The Teddy Bear People

T hey are all over the globe, they may have large collections or just a single bear, they hold rallies and Teddy Bears' picnics, they belong to one of several worldwide clubs, they may even write books on Teddies — all these people believe there is something special about the Teddy Bear.

Most agree that it is the Bear's serene air of acceptance, its way of listening to one's problems and staying calm in crises, that is so endearing. Many people have made great efforts to extend this benefit to others: Colonel Robert Henderson, the great Scottish collector; actor/author Peter Bull in England — and Russell A. McLean, "The Teddy Bear Man" of Lima, Ohio, in the USA.

Russell McLean was convinced that being given a Teddy would cheer up every child that was admitted to hospital in his home town, and he began a campaign, asking the public to send in their sales tax stamps to buy the toys. He achieved his aim: ever since, no child at Lima hospital has missed out on a Teddy Bear. Countless true stories prove that children in pain or fear are comforted by having a bear to hold. Before his death in 1969 The Teddy Bear Man had the joy of presenting Teddy number 50,000.

Bear Psychology

P sychologists have no trouble explaining the tie that binds a Teddy Bear to one who adores him. His animal shape, they say, reflects the archetypal images already in the unconscious, and stirs our imagination. We know instinctively the powerful fearsome aspect of the bear — like the hero Yu, strong enough to split mountains. At the same time, the warm softness of the Bear's fur, his cuddly size and his wordless comprehension of our needs confirm other images in our consciousness — of friendliness, affection and love.

Parents have no trouble understanding the Teddy's appeal, either, for they see these two aspects at work: a child's Teddy Bear is at once the alter ego, and the comforter. How often children will claim that Teddy has said or done things that express the child's own deep adventurous desires: the urge to say disobliging things about a grown-up, or to leap up from the ground and fly away, as one does in dreams. Then, when bedtime comes, Teddy is the soft, furry companion who keeps loneliness at bay.

Teddies do not need to be new or handsome — they just need to be there.

31

The Literary Bear

*Many artists and writers
who take the Teddy Bear for a theme
find ways to express that fierce,
pure love which belongs only
to childhood ...*

Three Cheers for Pooh

The world first met Winnie-the-Pooh when he came downstairs, bump, bump, bump, on the back of his head, behind Christopher Robin. Children have a way of turning things upside down, and A.A. Milne had a wonderful way of understanding them. By rights Christopher Robin's long-suffering toy should have been called Edward Bear, but in Chapter One of his endlessly delightful stories we learn that the name is Winnie-the-Pooh. And that's that. When pushed for an explanation, Christopher Robin replies scornfully, "Don't you know what *ther* means?"

Pooh lives in the woods where the little boy walks every day, but he is also Christopher Robin's very own bear. He has a busy life and friends, and adventures all his own, and at the same time he is always at hand to be talked to, dragged into escapades, bossed about and admonished: "Silly old bear!"

Thanks to A.A. Milne's wit and imagination, and E.H. Shepard's artistry, Pooh now belongs to us all, and no one will ever take his place.

Rupert and the Secret Paths

No Bear has ever been more blithely adventurous than Rupert, nor had a more obliging Mummy and Daddy. On the very brink of danger, he just tells them, "I'm waiting to see if a certain thing's going to happen. Please don't ask me what. It's terribly secret, but I'll tell you someday."

They never do ask, and the adventure always happens. The deceptively safe village of Nutwood, with its meadows, woods and Common, is alive with magic and mystery, and any hedgerow may hide a new path that only Rupert can discover.

This little bear is every child's dream of daring and freedom: he climbs, he digs, he explores far afield, goes out in all weathers, creeps outside at night with a torch — and is repaid for this boldness by breathtaking rides to castles in the clouds, and the promise of tea and buns when he returns home, jaunty and unscathed.

The fact that Rupert takes to the air so often is partly explained by the fact that Mary Tourtel, who created him for the *Daily Express* in 1920, was herself an aviator and adventurer. She illustrated his exploits until 1935, then Alfred Bestall took him up for another thirty years. A team of artists now produces the Rupert comic-strip and this famous Teddy Bear continues on his intrepid way.

The Bear in Boots

The germ of an idea which later became Paddington occurred to Michael Bond on Christmas Eve in 1956, when he was doing some late shopping, and noticed a Teddy Bear sitting alone on a shelf. He bought him at once, and two years later he saw the first Paddington book launched.

"He's not a cuddly bear," says Michael Bond. "He's a bear for standing up in a corner. That's why he wears Wellington boots."

There is something gruff and determined about Paddington, perhaps a little of true bearishness — but at the same time there is an endearing quality, a hint of dependence that makes one want to pick him up, even if cuddling is frowned upon. His famous label, *PLEASE LOOK AFTER THIS BEAR*, is after all rather a give-away.

A Teddy with a Purpose

S mokey Bear toys are available all over the United States and his face is known to millions. A tireless promoter, he appears in newspapers and magazines across the whole country. He is always on the campaign trail, fighting for a single cause — the preservation of America's forests from the danger of fire.

Smokey is a protector, and his clear message encourages children to be protectors also, by becoming Junior Forest Rangers and understanding the value of the natural environment and its countless families of creatures, all dependent on one another.

In his way, Smokey is an inheritor of that instinct for mutual survival shown by Teddy Roosevelt when he refused to shoot the bear in the Mississippi woods.

Aloysius

I n a story where most of the characters are intent on grabbing and holding onto their little bits of England, Sebastian Flyte, the well-born young exquisite in *Brideshead Revisited* (the novel by Evelyn Waugh) lives by different impulses. He is a student at Oxford, but he thinks more of his Teddy Bear, Aloysius, than he does of his studies. Faithful, understanding, petted and scolded by turns, Aloysius goes everywhere with Sebastian, riding in his open-seater Morris Cowley, enjoying a holiday with him in Italy and later travelling further abroad with his young master.

Just as Sebastian is both spoiled and strangely neglected, so is Aloysius: he has his own ivory-backed hairbrush, with "Aloysius" engraved on it, but the forgetful Sebastian is still capable of leaving him in a cab one night on the way home to college.

In the end, however, Aloysius is really just like other Teddies: mistreated sometimes, but nonetheless adored.

A Bear Anthology

*A celebration
of Teddies in verse ...*

Night Bears

BY WILMA HORSBRUGH

Three little bears
From nowhere in particular,
　　nowhere at all,
Came up the stairs
And climbed the perpendicular,
　　climbed the perpendicular,
　　nursery wall.

They sat upon the ceiling
And sang with all their might
Songs so full of feeling
They lasted half the night.

A funny thing it seemed
For little bears to do.
I think I must have dreamed
Those little bears, don't you?

For when the songs were ended
Then down the walls they slid,
And when they had descended
Do you know what they did?

Those three little bears
Went nowhere in particular,
   nowhere in particular,
   flat or or perpendicular,
   nowhere at all.

My Teddy Bear

By Jeffrey S. Forman

Lines written to celebrate the bear's
seventy - fifth birthday

He sits upon his pillowed throne
   A joyous smile upon his face.
And though his ears might seem outgrown
He carries them with pride and grace.

He's never cross or quick to carp
A friend in need he is to me.

When human tongues are mean and sharp
My teddy gives me sympathy.

To him I always bare my soul.
He lifts me when I'm feeling low.
And when I brag and miss my goal
He never says, 'I told you so.'

My friends may titter gleefully
And some may tease, but I don't care.
I hope that I will never be
Too old to love my Teddy bear.

Furry Bear

BY A.A. MILNE

If I were a bear,
    And a big bear too,
I shouldn't much care
        If it froze or snew;
I shouldn't much mind
        If it snowed or friz—
I'd be all fur-lined
        With a coat like his!

For I'd have fur boots and a brown fur wrap,
And brown fur knickers and a big fur cap,
I'd have a fur muffle-ruff to cover my jaws,
And brown fur mittens on my big brown paws.
With a big brown furry-down up to my head,
I'd sleep all the winter in a big fur bed.

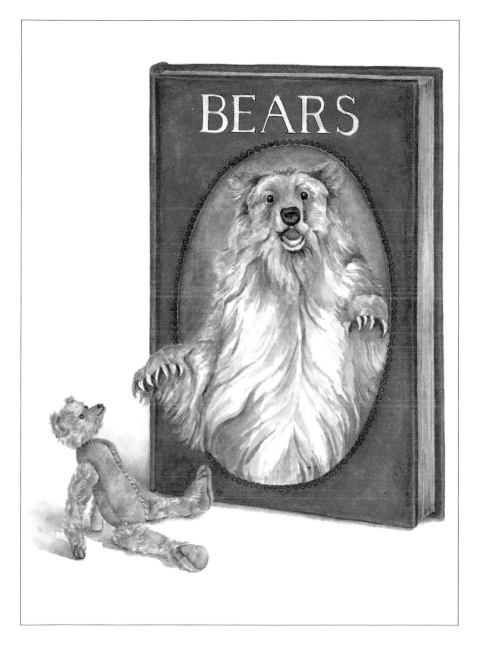

Archie

By Sir John Betjeman

Safe were those evenings in the pre-war world
When firelight shone on green linoleum;
I heard the church bells hollowing out the sky,
Deep beyond deep, like never-ending stars,
And turned to Archibald, my safe old bear,
Whose woollen eyes looked sad or glad at me,
Whose ample forehead I could wet with tears,
Whose half-moon ears received my confidence,
Who made me laugh, who never let me down.
I used to wait for hours to see him move,
Convinced that he could breathe. One dreadful day
They hid him from me as punishment:
Sometimes the desolation of that loss
Comes back to me and I must go upstairs
To see him in the sawdust, so to speak,
Safe and returned to his idolator.

From *Summoned by Bells*

Rare Bears

This bear, made by Chiltern
of England in the 1930s,
was taken to Guernsey and then to
New Zealand and Australia.
The music box under his
muff still plays.
All over the world there are
bears with rare
tales to tell ...

Peter the Rarest Bear

F rom the days when early men fought the great cave bears of the past, these powerful animals have appeared in the old European stories; and in later centuries, the bear was still a popular figure in folk tales. By speaking of him in this way, humans tried to tame this fabulous beast in their minds, so that terror was turned into affection, and fear into trust and love. The gentle, protective bear became legend, and was eventually transformed into a soft, warm creature that even children could hold in their arms.

That is why Peter the Bear is now rare, for he was made in the late 1920s in the town of Neustadt, and he had a fierce face, rolling glass eyes, a wicked tongue, and two rows of pointy wooden teeth. Add to that his realistic growl, which he sometimes came out with while still in his toybox, and no wonder no one wanted to buy him and take him home.

Alas, poor Peter — lonely but not forgotten, he is now the rarest Teddy Bear in the world.

*Fearsome Peter, an unusual antique, is
drawn here from "life".*

The Most
Audacious Bear

We do not expect Teddy Bears to be cheeky or pert —
somehow they seem too wise and benevolent for that —
but there was an early bear who proved himself particularly
bold. He belonged to Mr Walter Pelham, who was a young
man at Trinity College, Cambridge, when President Roosevelt
visited there in 1905.

This audacious bear raised not a murmur of protest when
Walter and a friend decided to lower him on a string to
confront "Teddy" Roosevelt as he passed beneath their
college windows.

Outwardly calm, but no doubt with a thumping heart,
Teddy swooped downward on his string and hovered inches
from the startled president's nose. The great man stopped,
raised his hand, then shook the paw of the little bear.

Only another Teddy could guess what words might have
passed between the two on that historic occasion.

The Fastest Bear on Land or Water

M r Woppit first appeared as a character in the children's comic, *Robin,* in 1953. The deputy editor later came to know the great Donald Campbell, and had Mr Woppit made as a present for the famous speedsman. The little bear became his mascot, and travelled in the cockpit of his vehicle whenever he tried for a speed record.

Donald Campbell and Mr Woppit made it in May 1959 on Coniston Water, breaking the world's water speed record at 260.3 miles per hour in the streamlined Bluebird.

In Utah the next year they both came through the fastest car crash in history: Campbell ended up in hospital, but Mr Woppit survived with only a dented nose.

Their great feat was pushing the land speed record to 403 miles per hour.

Then, sadly, Donald Campbell was killed in a crash on Coniston Water in January 1967. Mr Woppit, found floating in the lake, went home to Mrs Campbell, and his flamboyant and faithful racing life came to an end.

Musical Bears

The most famous tune
for Teddies...

The Teddy Bears' Picnic

WORDS BY JIMMY KENNEDY
MUSIC BY JOHN W. BRATTON

If you go down in the woods today
You're sure of a big surprise
If you go down in the woods today
You'd better go in disguise;
For every bear that ever there was
Will gather there for certain, because
Today's the day the Teddy Bears have their picnic.

Every Teddy Bear who's been good
Is sure of a treat today.
There's a lot of marvellous things to eat,
And wonderful games to play.
Beneath the trees where nobody sees
They'll hide and seek as
long as they please,
'Cause that's the way the
Teddy Bears have
their picnic.

If you go down in the woods today
You'd better not go alone.
It's lovely down in the woods today
But safer to stay at home.
For every Bear that ever there was
Will gather there for certain, because
Today's the day the Teddy Bears have their picnic.

Picnic time for Teddy Bears
The little Teddy Bears are having a lovely time today.
Watch them, catch them unawares
And see them picnic on their holiday.
See them gaily gad about,
They love to play and shout,
They never have any care;
At six o'clock their Mummies and Daddies
Will take them home to bed,
Because they're tired little Teddy Bears.

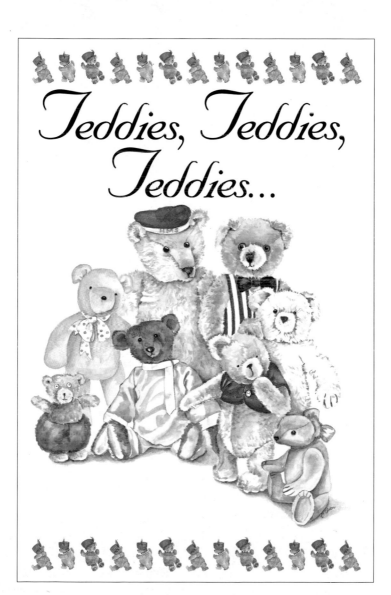

Teddies, Teddies, Teddies...

Bears by the Lake

I f you should happen to visit England's beautiful Lake
District, you may be honoured by a chance meeting with
the newest mysterious inhabitants of the uplands and fells.
The dramatic landscapes that were once the inspiration for the
poet Wordsworth and the Romantics are the magical home of
the Lakeland Bear families.

These are country bears, at one with the hills and valleys,
wrapped up against the chill in traditional woollen sweaters
and Herdwick tweed, and wearing leather clogs upon their
furry feet. Busy as the bees that make the local heather honey,
the Lakeland bears are farmers, rangers and foresters, happy
in a region green with oaks and chestnuts, and inhabited still
by red squirrels.

Some Lakeland bears go backpacking, and should you
meet them on a highland track, they may share a crumble of
mintcake with you, or lend you a walking stick (very useful if
you happen to be like them - 18 inches tall). Then, in the wink
of an eyelid, the little creatures will vanish into the mist,
leaving behind a hint of Lakeland mystery.

The Amazing Dancing Bear

In Russia once an Empress reigned:
Elizabeth, famed for her jewels and dresses,
    A devotee of fine champagne,
With mischievous eyes, and abundant gold tresses.

    Saint Petersburg one winter was chill:
The Empress flung wide all her windows and doors,
    The Neva flooded over the sill
And froze overnight on the smooth palace floors.

    There never was a party since
Where the beauties, the music or wine could compare;
    Much to the joy of every prince
The delight of the night was a dancing black bear.

    He took to the ice on silver skates,
Pirouetted and whirled with incredible speed,
    He juggled baubles and golden plates,
In all of the dancing the bear took the lead.

    His midnight fur, his eyes so bright
In the colourful throng glittered everywhere
    And no one ever forgot the night
When the Empress invited the dancing bear.

An Indian Love Chant

In the mountains, by the rivers,
Lived the bears of ancient story,
Lived and hunted, loved and married,
Told their cubs of tribal glory.

One bear tale among the many
Sang of Furry Bear and White Dove,
Bears who yearned to be together,
Bears whose parents dimmed their bright love.

Rigid was the parents' honour,
Fatal was the parents' anger:
Never were the two to marry,
Even touching paws spelt danger.

By a wigwam, all in secret,
Furry Bear met little White Dove.
Each in joy and proud defiance
Swore their passion was the right love.

Then they pledged eternal union,
Joined their paws, sped to the river,
Plunged together, kissed, and perished:
So their love goes on for ever.

Teddy Bear Biscuits

Ａll you need to begin with is a biscuit cutter in the shape of a Teddy Bear, and a sweet tooth.

❧

INGREDIENTS

125g butter or margarine
60g sugar
3 heaped teaspoons condensed milk
a few drops of vanilla essence
200g flour
1 teaspoon baking powder
1 teaspoon cinnamon
30g dark chocolate chips
1 small egg

❧

METHOD

Cream the butter, sugar and condensed milk, and add the essence.

Add the dry ingredients and chocolate chips.

Add enough of the beaten egg to make a stiff mixture.

Roll out gently on a floured board to 0.5cm thickness

and cut with biscuit cutter.
Place on a cold, greased tray and bake 20
minutes at 190°C.

Any small bear will be delighted to help you eat these
biscuits, and without much prompting will finish off the
leftover condensed milk.

"My True Love Hath My Heart ..."

M y true love hath my heart, and I have his,
By just exchange one for the other given.
I hold his dear, and mine he cannot miss;
There never was a better bargain driven.
His heart in me keeps me and him in one;
He loves my heart, for once it was his own;
I cherish his, because in me it bides.

SIR PHILIP SYDNEY

Acknowledgements

The publisher is grateful to the following for permission to reproduce copyright material or to represent a copyright image: page 37 Express Newspapers PLC; 39 Lemon, Unna and Durbridge Ltd; 46 Wilma Horsbrugh: 50 "Furry Bear" by A.A. Milne, published by Methuen Children's Books; 52 "Archie" by John Betjeman, John Murray (Publishers) Ltd; 64 & 66 The Teddy Bears' Picnic, words by Jimmy Kennedy, music by John W. Bratton, © Copyright 1907 M. Witmark and Sons, New York (Allans Music Australia Pty Ltd, P.O. Box C156, Cremorne Junction, NSW 2090 Australia).Thanks are also extended to Yvonne Tonnison and The Teddy Bear Shop,Double Bay, Sydney, Australia; and to the Lakeland Bear Co, England.

The publisher has made every effort to trace copyright holders. If we have inadvertently omitted to acknowledge anyone, we should be most grateful if this could be brought to our attention.

A Kevin Weldon Production
Published by Weldon Publishing
a division of Kevin Weldon and Associates
Level 5, 70 George Street Sydney, NSW 2000, Australia

First published in 1992

© Copyright: Kevin Weldon and Associates Pty Limited 1992
© Copyright design: Kevin Weldon and Associates Pty Limited 1992

Illustrated by Rosalie Upton
Text by Cheryl A. Hingley
Designed by Denese Cunningham
Printed by South China Printing Co Ltd, Hong Kong

National Library of Australia Cataloguing-in-Publication data

Upton, Rosalie
A gift book of teddy bears.

ISBN 1 86302 232 5.

1. Teddy bears — Miscellanea I. Title.

688.724